Mirror
To the
Soul
Of a
Woman

To: Josephine
Thanks
Barbara

Poems by

Gloria Murphy Smith

[AP]

Published by:

[AP]
Amani Publishing
P. O. Box 12045
Tallahassee, FL 32317-2045

A publishing company based on faith, hope, and love

Visit our website at: www.Barbarajoewilliams.com

E-mail us at: Amanipublishing@aol.com
Or e-mail Gloria Murphy Smith at: Glomsmith19736@aol.com

Printed in the United States of America

ISBN: 0975285149

Library of Congress Control Number: 2006926002

Cover photograph courtesy of: Istockphoto.com

Dedication

This book is dedicated to the loving memory of my grandmother, Anna Brookins Hendry, who has always been a positive role model and inspiration in my life. Though you are no longer with me physically, your spirit lives on forever.

It is also dedicated to my aunt, Christine Murphy Fuqua, who adopted my sisters, my brother and me, after the death of our mother when we were infants and toddlers. These two women instilled in me all the positive things that have made me what I am today. Continue to rest in peace until we meet again.

Foreword

By
Dr. Vera J. Roberts
District Content Specialist/Advisor Social Science/ History K-12
Lynwood Unified School District
Los Angeles, California

Gloria Murphy Smith is a gifted and talented writer. Her poetry awakens joy, pain, and suffering in the reader through her creative expression. She became seriously ill and resigned from her position at Florida A&M University in May 2001. Gloria took the excruciating pain of her illness and began to pour out her spirit through the writing of poetry.

Mirror to the Soul of a Woman is a storybook of inspiration for leaders and teachers. The book is easy to reference by contemporary themes. Through it all, Gloria's inspirational and motivational poems are treasures of wisdom that mirror the experiences of her life, community, and nation.

Table of Contents

The Love of a Daughter
What I Wouldn't Give
You'll Always Have My Trust

Relationships
All That You Can
Free At Last
I Am a Woman
I Can't Let Go
If You Could Read My Mind
I'm In Love
Is It Too Much to Ask
It Could've Been You
It Is Time to Move On
I Wonder
I Would Like to Believe
Let's Follow Our Heart
Let's Make a Deal
Love Is
Love Is Just a Fairy Tale
Love Is Like a Flower
Love Is Not a Game We Play
My Baby's Father
My Friend, My Lover
My Love Is Stone Cold
My Mind Is Too Deep
No Coming Back
Now Ain't the Time
Now That You Are Gone
Once In a While
Only You Can Make This Dream Come True
Roll In the Hay
So Many Times
There Are No More Tears to Shed
There Was a Time
The Two of Us
This Heart's For You
Too Hard to Bear
You Are My Destiny
You Must Take a Chance
You're My Boo

Spiritual

Did You Remember
First and Foremost In My Life
Freedom for All
God Is Just
God Is Not Pleased
God Promised
I Am Going to a Better Resting Place
I Believe in Jesus
I Can Always Turn to Jesus
I Don't Care What Nobody Says
I Foresee a Better Tomorrow
I Know of a Home
I'll Be Waiting at God's Gate
I Love You Lord
I Need You Lord
I Want to Be Ready
Just Let Me Enjoy This Peace
Leave Everything to God
Let Us All Make a Difference
Lord, Please Forgive Me
Lord, Why Me?
My Talk With Jesus
My Testimony
Nothing In Life Is a Guarantee
One Day My Troubles Will Be Over
Prayer Is the Answer
Striving for That Spiritual Being
The Power of Prayer
Why Must We Obey the Gospel?
You Must Hold On

About the Author
Acknowledgements

Emotional Rollercoaster

A DEDICATION TO JOHNNIE COCHRAN

Johnnie Cochran was a man
That we all respected,
He made sure that his clients
Were never neglected

When you needed an attorney
He was the man to call,
He fought to have justice
To serve us all

He wasn't just known
For winning the O.J. case,
He fought for our civil rights
In so many ways

When he went out in public
He knew just how to dress,
I really don't believe
He'd have settled for anything less

He had a smile that would win you over
And make you melt in your seat,
He was an attorney that others
Had trouble trying to defeat

I'm not going to say
That I knew the man well,
But for all of those who did
Have only great things to tell

Johnnie, when you took the O.J. case
All eyes were on you,
For nine whole months
I was stuck to the television like glue

No matter how tough the case
He was never backed in a corner,
Johnnie was a man
Of such great honor

He stood tall in his suits
With much dignity,
And thought the world would be a better place
Without the bigotry

Always in the courtroom
He was very diplomatic,
Though his opponents may have seen him
As being too problematic

Although his life was cut short
He put up a good fight,
I've never heard any one say
That he didn't treat them right

My heart goes out to his family
And I have sympathy for his wife,
I only wish that God would have
Let him live a much longer life.

A HOME BY THE BAY

This is such a
Beautiful day,
With all the little ones
Going out to play
The flowers are green
And in full bloom,
There is absolutely
No more gloom

No clouds in the sky
And the sun shining bright,
Late at night
The moon is full of light
When the sun goes down
And the stars come out,
It's just all so beautiful
Without a doubt

The birds flying high
Across the sky,
Spreading their beautiful wings,
Some just learning to fly
The beaches are full
And the water is just right,
And everyone is filled
With joy and delight

I open the windows
And in come the fresh air,
Then go for a drive with
The wind blowing through my hair
Spring is now here
And it's such a beautiful day,
It's always been my dream
To own a home by the bay.

ALWAYS THINK TWICE

Always think twice
Before you speak,
Try not to say things
That you know are weak

If you can't bring yourself
To say something nice,
Remember that one day
You may have to pay the price

Don't just say things
If you believe they're not so,
Repeat only those things
That you truly know

When you find yourself thinking that
You might take some heat,
Always think twice
Before you speak

Always remember
To tell the truth,
This is something you should have
Been taught as a youth

And when there is something
You feel you must leak,
Remember to think twice
Before you speak.

A YOUNG BLACK MAN

When a young black man
Is stunned with a gun,
And the police say
He was trying to run

Instead of confessing
To their mistake,
A criminal case
They'll try to make

When these police know
Deep in their heart ,
That this young man
Did not take part

We must find a way
To set him free,
Passing laws to protect
Innocent people like you and me

He needs to know
That he'll be protected,
No more of his rights
Will be rejected

When he did not do
What they say he did,
These corrupt police
We must get rid

They'll make up things
To fit their need,
Even if it means doing
Some dirty deed

He feels the only thing left to do
Is to take the stand,
And realize that the rest
Is in God's hand

When this young man
Is no more than a youth,
But is condemned
For telling the truth

We can't walk away
And turn our head,
Because too many of them
Already are dead.

DON'T LET YOURSELF GO

When you're adding on a pound
And your body's looking round,
Make yourself glow
Don't let yourself go

If you're holding your head down
You feel you're looking like a clown,
Let everybody know
Don't let yourself go

If you're always wearing a frown
Or walking around in your gown,
Stop feeling low
Don't let yourself go

When you sit down at the table
And no one thinks you're able,
Give their minds a blow
Don't let yourself go.

HOW MANY TIMES MUST A BLACK MAN DIE

How many times
Must a black man die?
Why do we always assume
He's telling a lie?

From the time he's old enough
To try to do his best,
The police are waiting
To put him under arrest

While he's driving along the highway
Just enjoying the view,
The number of policemen that stop him
Is more than a few

They jump out of their cars,
Shooting without any regards,
They don't care how many lives
They have caused to be scarred

When they've taken away his dignity
And he is left with no pride,
He knows that the law is never
Going to be on his side

When it is captured on video
As plain as day,
But somehow the police still manage
To explain it their way

When we all see the bullets
That's ringing through the air,
And the man is just sitting there
With a blank stare

They want us to believe
They were just doing their job,
But we can all see they were
Acting more like the mob

We've often wondered why
A black man would try to flee,
Now we know that if he doesn't,
He won't live to make his plea

When the media see what's happening
And chooses to become overjoyed,
They never stop to think
That others just might be annoyed

When they don't have to pay
For the damage they've done,
They know they've gotten away,
And again they've won

When this black man has done
Everything he could to comply,
Just how many times
Must a black man die?

IT IS NOT OKAY

It is not okay
To disown your race,
Or forget where you come from
And not know your place

It is not okay
To pretend that you are white,
Being born in a family
That has always been black

It is not okay
To forget who you are,
Not remembering those
Who made you a star

It is not okay
To look like a clown,
Bleaching your skin white
Just to keep from being brown

It is not okay
To be accused of molesting boys,
Just because you took them in
And gave them all toys

It is not okay
To be the center of everyone's joke,
Make sure your attorney
Find some holes to poke

It is not okay
To put your family through this hell,
Flying around the world
Looking like Tinker Bell

It is not okay
If you didn't have the sense to ban
Any human being
Who thought he was Peter Pan

It is not okay
To do an illegal search,
When you've been waiting
Like a bird sitting on his perch

It is not okay
To try and build a case,
Or get revenge on someone
Because you don't like their race

It is not okay
To be using taxpayers money,
Laughing in the media
Like the whole ordeal is funny

It is not okay
To play with someone else's life,
When you only brought these charges
Because you already had some strife.

IT ONLY TAKES A PLAN

It only takes a plan
To stay on the right track,
And when you begin to understand
You won't be taken aback

Sometimes you must listen
To what others have to say,
Although you may be one to glisten
You can't always do as you may

You must learn to take a stand
And also get up and fight,
Don't be afraid to make a demand
As long as it is done right

It takes more than just a number
To prove that you're a man,
So wake up and do not slumber
For it only takes a plan.

IT'S JUST A MATTER OF TIME

It's just a matter of time
Before Al-Quaeda strikes again,
But before we try to mastermind,
We must surely come up with a plan

While our leaders are steady lying,
I know that we all can guess,
Our children are somewhere dying
And they're still here making a mess

Last time we had no clue
Of when or where the enemy would hit,
This time they'll get what's due
And they deserve every bit

We must all be on alert
And we must keep our eyes wide open,
While some feel the need to desert,
Others are there only for the token

We can not be caught slipping
Or sleeping with both eyes shut,
For Al-Quaeda will be tipping,
And searching through every rut

To keep this country free,
Pretty soon we won't have a dime,
But the whole world is able to see
It's just a matter of time.

LEARN TO HAVE RESPECT

We have been known to make an assumption
Of the things we don't really know,
And many times there have been much consumption
So many good things we decided to blow

We always find a way to not give credit
Although it is well deserved,
We'll take the time to be sure and edit
And pretend it was already reserved

There may come a time when we have to compete
And cause one another to become annoyed,
But we try so hard to find a way to defeat
We forget this was a time we could have enjoyed

Don't be one to take things too serious
For we must find a way to unite,
And don't be one to become so furious
We cause the problem to ignite

We must all use our own discretion
To make sure everyone is treated fair,
So many times we'll get the wrong impression
So many times we seem not to care

If we don't do the things that others expect
And we ask them to give us their vote,
We may end up losing their respect
For they'll make sure to save every quote.

LET ME SMELL MY ROSES

All throughout the years
My life's been full of tears,
It's no fun to be a cripple
Though I'm not like Jack the Ripple

I want to be back in classes
And attend my Sunday masses,
I know when my door closes
I'll never smell my roses

I want to take my time
I'm not asking for a dime,
While I still have my noses
Just let me smell my roses

Don't wait till it's too late
Then I can't appreciate,
I've taken so many doses
Please let me smell my roses

The time is getting near
One thing I do not fear,
Like God took care of Moses
He'll let me smell my roses.

MATERIAL THINGS

Just because you're riding
In a new navigator,
You think you can rule the world
Like some dictator,
And just because you're wearing
A big diamond ring,
This is only
A material thing

When you won the lottery
And became a millionaire,
You started dancing around
Like Fred Astaire,
Listen to this song
I'm trying to sing,
This is only
A material thing

Spending so much money
Taking women out to Vegas,
And going to different stores
Buying all the toy Segas,
It's time to stop now
You've had your little fling,
This is only
A material thing

When you got on the road
In your Cadillac truck,
You didn't think for once
You might run out of luck,
I feel very sorry
You went out with a bang,
But those were only
Material things!

MIRROR TO THE SOUL OF A WOMAN

What I see when I look in the mirror
Goes so much deeper than just the bare skin,
It takes me to a place that's so much nearer
To all the things I have built up within,
I keep searching through my soul
Wondering if I am all that I can be,
I keep looking in the mirror
Wondering is there anything left for me to see

When I look into the mirror
I do it with calm and with ease,
It helps me to see things so much clearer
It leads me to know that life has no guarantees,
What the mirror can see goes so very deep
And after all, it does not lie,
The things that are in my mind are so very steep
The mirror can make me laugh, and it can also cause me to cry

The mirror lets me know if I am up to par
It is a reflection of who I am,
Though it does not determine who we are
We can be sure it is not a scam,
If the mirror could talk, there would be a lot that it could say
It would let me know if there is any more hope,
For it does not discriminate between night and day
It is like looking at me through a microscope

There are so many things the mirror can tell
About the mind of me as a whole,
And the things I need to excel
For the mirror does not play just some minor role,
When I'm searching through my soul
For the answers that are yet to come,
I know just how to take control
From the mirror to the soul of a woman.

MY PAIN

(Written by my daughter, LaChanda Brooks)

Tears of joy, tears all the time
My pain is here, I can't define
No one understands, no one cares
My pain is here, too hard to share

I open one door, another one is closed
I try so hard, but no one knows
I write on paper, it's easy to say
But no one knows the pain I feel all day

Can anyone hear me, does anyone care?
Don't worry they say, your family is here
My pain it hurts, and I can't seem to hide
I just wish I had someone on my side

Where do I look, who can I call?
Only GOD Himself can break this wall
I ask of Him to show me the way
GOD, You know my pain I feel all day

Keep in mind on this short, short note
My pain is here, and I just can't cope
Help me Lord Jesus, hear my plea
Grant me the strength to have faith in Thee!

OPRAH, I'M YOUR BIGGEST FAN

Oprah, my lady,
You are the best,
Your work stands out
From all the rest

Each and every day
When I watch your show,
You walk out on stage
With such dignity and glow

Some love you
Because you're famous
Others because you're rich,
I love you because you're you
And handle yourself well
Without ever a glitch

Every now and then
When you give away a car,
I think to myself
She really lives up to par

I saw you on Biography
And I watch all your movies too,
And no one else could've ever played
In the Color Purple like you

When you went to court in Texas
For the Mad Cow Disease,
I knew you'd win the case
That was nothing but a tease

You're an inspiration to all
Who wants to lose weight,
For someone like me
Who feels I'm carrying freight,
And for all the people in Africa
That you've done so much good,
I'm sure they thank you dearly
For supporting their neighborhood

You bring glamour to show biz
And you really set the stage,
And remember all those best sellers,
I've read every page

In order to meet you
I do all that I can,
'Cause I want you to know, Oprah
That I'm your biggest fan!

PIECE OF THE PIE

I was left all alone
And cut to the bone,
I was willing to die
For my piece of the pie

I climbed real high
I couldn't take a sigh,
Who said I couldn't have
My piece of the pie.

I got good grades
And I thought I had it made,
I just want what's mine
And that's my piece of the pie

I would get up at night
Before day was in sight,
Why shouldn't I have
Just my piece of the pie?

I stayed up late
Working for my mate,
I only want my
Piece of the pie.

RAW DEAL
Dedicated to Terri Schiavo

Everyone should have
The right to die,
Though we should not have to do it
Because of a lie

Who said that your life
Is greater than mine?
Removing one's feeding tube
Is crossing the line

Just because she isn't
Someone that you love,
Does not give you the right
To pull the plug

Terri's husband is hiding
Behind our laws,
But that doesn't mean
He doesn't have any flaws

This is a murder in which
Our government took part,
The doctors, the lawyers and Judges
None of which has a heart

I hope this will show the world
That we have no say,
To put these people in office
It really doesn't pay

How can anyone
Be so cruel?
This is no different
From having a duel

We won't listen to what
Terri's parents have to say,
But we'll put people in jail
For treating animals this way

We turn on the television
And see such a shameful sight,
So give praise to her family
For putting up a good fight

We can only sit and wonder
How her parents must feel,
Because they truly have been given
A very raw deal!

STATE OF DEPRESSION

I have trouble falling asleep
And no appetite to eat,
I've learned one hard lesson
I'm in a state of depression

I don't talk on the phone,
I'd rather be alone,
What's your suggestion?
I'm in a state of depression

I can't go out and play
In my house I just stay,
I have no affection
I'm in a state of depression

If it shows on my face
I've lost all of my grace,
It's in my reflection
I'm in a state of depression

I never go for a drive
I hardly feel alive,
I have no expression
I'm in a state of depression.

THE DAY AMERICA CAME TO A HALT

In the twinkle of an eye
Our world fell apart,
On that bright, sunny morning
In America's New York

While some of us were sleeping
Others busy at work,
Our enemy was creeping, sneaking
Sheepishly planning how to
destroy our beautiful soil

Though you might have destroyed
a very significant number of our heroes
There will always be a
memorial in their honor
For the world to see at Ground Zero!

When you wake up one day
Osama Bin Laden
You'll wish you had taken time to pray,
Instead of spreading your hatred and
sending your assassins to take our joy away

When you took down our plane
At the famous Pentagon,
Killing men, women, and children
with no regards

You made a mistake
of how vulnerable we could be
By bringing America to a halt,
But we're quickly coming after ye!

And though you killed many more
In rural Pennsylvania,
The Lord Almighty was with us
But who will be with you
When America comes to hang ya?

Only evil and cowards
who will never show their faces,
Will you be able to succumb to
In some dangerous places

So run while you can
Because you're not a man,
To find someone like you
It only takes a plan

So that day will never be forgotten
On September 11, 2001,
When you made Americans
stronger and closer
By making each of us a hero,
And spreading our love
For each other at Ground Zero!

THE RIGHT TO LIVE

Dedicated to Terri Schiavo

We've all talked about
The right to die,
But what about
The right to live?
We'll never know
Who is telling the lie,
So her feeding tube
We must give

It could be your loved one
In this situation,
Or it could
Very well be mine
Our political leaders
Have failed us,
And from all indication,
They care more about where
They're going out to dine

Terri was once
A beautiful lady,
And as vibrant
As she could be
Her life was cut short
Before having her first baby,
Now she's depending
On you and me

To let everyone know
That we don't have a heart,
It really doesn't take very much
But now is the time
For us all to take part,
Writing letters to
Our Congress and such

One of these days
You might regret your decision,
After all it could be
Your turn next
God forbid if you should lose
All of your vision,
And can no longer
Read any text

Will you wish then
That you had done your best,
To fight to do God's will?
It could've been your vote
That put this matter to rest,
For we all should have
The right to live!

TIME IS TOO SHORT

Time is too short
For us to be at war,
Ours soldiers should not be fighting
In a country that far,
Before we try to take care
Of someone else's home,
There should be no discrepancies
In our own

We have yet to be told
Why we must fight,
Though you want us to believe
That you are right,
We don't always know
Who we may need,
Try and think twice
Before you plant your seed

We live in a country
That's always been free,
Now we've gotten ourselves involved
With the devil for an enemy,
We need to spend more time
Finding a way to make peace,
So no other soldier
Will ever have to decease

God is not pleased
With the way these things are run,
We must lean on Jesus
Who is God's Son,
We may wake up one day
And get a surprise,
For this might be the time
For our demise.

VIOLENCE IS NOT THE ANSWER

Violence is not the answer
No matter what we may think,
The more we try to embrace it
The more our lives will sink

Violence is not the answer
There are other things that we must do,
When we settle our disputes through violence
We create more problems for me and you

Violence is not the answer
Of how we must defend,
When you took the oath to lead us
It's on you our lives depend

Violence is not the answer
When you feel the need for revenge,
We must come up with a better solution
For life to go on without a hinge

Violence is not the answer
When you want to settle a score,
For when it comes time to pay the price
We lose our lives forever more.

WE NEED GREAT LEADERS

There should never be a need for retaliation
We need to focus more on our students' education,
And when we take a look at our schools retention
We need to find a way to deal with student suspension

There are so many things that we need to improve
And so-called leaders that we need to remove,
And when it comes to qualification
Leaders should me made to show verification

We have so many bridges that we need to cross
The first thing we need to do is find the right boss,
We need to find leaders who have our students concern
Someone whom we know is willing to return

When a leader doesn't show some gratification
This would be the time for ratification,
We need leaders that'll make sure our students excel
Not those that are there just to find a reason to expel

Someone who won't run away when the going gets tough
And who is willing to stay when things get rough,
There comes a time when we must negate
Find great leaders that we can validate.

WHO GIVES US THE RIGHT TO KILL?

Dedicated To Terri Schiavo

So many times we have trusted
The Court of Appeals,
Now they're removing our tubes
And stopping our meals,
Though they make their laws
And force them into bills,
Who gives us
The right to kill?

She could see, she could hear,
And she has a brain,
This has put her family
Under enormous strain,
We'll never know
How much pain she can feel,
So who gives us
The right to kill?

Send her home to her mother
Or maybe even to her brother,
Not to her husband, not the Judge,
Nor no other,
It doesn't take much to see
That this woman is real,
Who gives us
The right to kill?

How can anyone with a heart
Bear to pull this tube?
They must not have a conscience
And be down right crude,
There's no way for her family
To swallow this pill,

Who gives us
The right to kill?

Our country has failed
To fill their obligation,
The doctors seem to have trouble
With corroboration,
Has the husband made
Some kind of a deal?
Who gives us
The right to kill?

Her mother and father were the ones
Who gave her life,
Not some cold fellow who said
She was his wife,
We all know
This is not God's will,
So who gives us
The right to kill?

The courts should be made
For our legal defense,
To commit this murder
Makes no good sense,
If you read your Bible
You would know His will,
He never gave us
The right to kill

Where is the justice
In this democracy?
When all our leaders
Are practicing hypocrisy,
Terri should be given
Every chance there is to live,
But we do not have
The right to kill!

YOU CAN'T SAVE THE WORLD

When you've done all you can
And have God in your plan,
Take a step back
And try to relax

When you've kept all your engages
And covered all your pages,
Just like Raymond Burl
You can't save the world

When you've come to the end
And have no one to depend,
Try to let go
And take a back row

If things should go awry
And someone else begins to pry,
Don't just take a whirl
'Cause you can't save the world.

Family Ties

A HUSBAND IS NOT A HUSBAND

A husband is not a husband
When he can't leave his mother's arm,
Though he tries to come across
With personality and charm

When he refuses to take control
Because she causes such alarm,
He feels your only responsibility
Is to protect him from harm

To hear her say, he shouldn't give you respect
That's only for her and his sisters,
You realize then he's not a husband
So send him on his way with your best wishes.

ALL I CAN DO NOW IS PRAY FOR YOU

From the day you were born
And opened your big bright eyes,
I knew whatever you did in life
Would come as no surprise

There are so many great things
That a mother can do,
But the greatest thing of all
Is to pray for you

When you became a toddler
And wanted the best of every toy,
Those would be some of the best days
I would get to enjoy

As you became a small boy
And started acting more curious,
I had to pray really hard
To keep from becoming so furious

When you grew into a teenager
And could not have your own way,
I prayed day and night
That you would not go astray

Now that you've grown into a young man
With many decisions to make,
I hope you'll do the right thing,
If not for yourself, please, for God's sake

There were so many days
When my heart would bleed,
Those were the days
That I would beg and plead

There is no joy seeing you
In pain and distress,
So each and every issue
I would like you to address

When you made a mistake
And didn't know what to do,
My life was also affected
Because I felt the strain too

A child is born
And given a chance to live,
And his mother is there
To teach him how to forgive

There will soon come a time
When I won't be around,
Let there be nothing in your life
That will cause you to be hell-bound

When you were a small child
I did all I could do,
All I can do now
Is pray for you.

A MOTHER'S LOVE

I wish that you could see
All the love I have in my heart,
There's nothing I wouldn't do
To keep us from being apart

I knew that you were special
The moment you were conceived,
And when I held you in my arms
I couldn't be more relieved

Your father decided to leave us
To make himself free,
And left all the loving and caring for you
Completely up to me

I only want what's best for you
To make a good living,
And also to try and teach you
The meaning of forgiving

I'll work two jobs for you
Just to give you what you need,
And when it comes to guidance
I will always be in the lead

I'll do all the things that'll help you
To know that life is real,
And when you are sick
I'll be with you until you heal

To guarantee you an education
I did what it took,
But I couldn't break any rules
To get you off the hook

Not in a million years
Will I turn my back on you,
And I know that the Lord
Will always see us through

Don't ever get discouraged
Nor think that I don't care,
For the ones that tell you that
Are the ones you should beware

Except for the love that comes
From our precious God above,
There's nothing in this world
That's greater than a mother's love.

A SISTER LIKE YOU

To have a sister like you
Is not a common thing,
Because in my view
You're head of the ring

We grew up together
And went our separate ways,
But I'll love and cherish you
All of my days

To have a sister like you
Make me stop and realize,
What others take for granted
And how they theorize

When we talk on the phone
Or write an email,
You would think we'd never gone
But had a train derail

To have a sister like you
Is none less than the best,
Because you're like no other
It makes you greater than the rest.

I HAVE A STORY TO TELL

I have a story to tell
And I hope I can do it well,
Of how I searched my soul
In order to reach my goal

My life was not easy
Sometimes I became queasy,
But I knew what I had to do
To help get my children through

I'd walk a mile to the store
Sometimes even more,
But I would never beg
As long as I had a leg

I'd get up in the dark
And walk through the park,
To take my kids to school
So they'd be nobody's fool

I'd go to work every day
With very little time to play,
And when I got home each night
I'd make sure their homework was right

We didn't have much to eat
Or shoes to wear on our feet,
But one thing that we all knew
We had Jesus in our view

We always took time to pray
And hear what Jesus had to say,
For we knew that there would come a day
When our love for Him would surely pay.

IT'S OUR GOLDEN ANNIVERSARY

It's our golden anniversary
And there is no other place
That I'd rather be,
Than spending all of my time
Just loving you,
Doing everything that I can
To make your dreams come true

I've spent the past fifty years
With you on my mind,
Caring for you, sharing with you
And always being kind

From the first day we met
I knew that you were the one,
When I took your hand in marriage,
I knew God's work had been done

We've laughed and we've joked
And even cried a few tears,
We've been there for each other
All throughout the years

When I look into your eyes
I'm reminded of just how much we care,
And it brings back memories
Of all the small things we share

When we wake up in the mornings
And put breakfast on the table,
We remember to thank the Lord
For without Him we would not have been able

To conquer so many obstacles
That tried to stand in our way,
But they only brought us closer
For our love was here to stay

There are so many things
That I would like to say,
To show you how I feel
On this special day

But no amount of words
Nor the most expensive art,
Can begin to express to you
The joy I feel in my heart

We knew from the beginning
That our feelings were real,
And not one day has gone by
That you've lost that appeal

You brought joy into my life
In so many different ways,
I will love you and cherish you
For the rest of our days.

Happy golden anniversary my love!

LORD, PLEASE SAVE MY CHILD

I know that life
Hasn't always been good,
I tried to give you
All the love that I could

We're all at fault
Every once in a while,
I need you Lord Jesus
To save my child

Now you're all grown up
And making your own decisions,
I pray and ask God
To give you the right visions

I guess sometimes
I could've been in denial,
I turn to you Lord Jesus
To save my child

Because you made a mistake
Doesn't mean it's the end,
God wants you to know
It's on Him you need to depend

Stay out of the crowd
And start acting more mild,
Please, Lord Jesus,
Save my child

I can't sleep at night
For wondering if you're alright,
Get up in the morning
Sometimes losing my sight

I live each day
Praying you won't run wild,
I'm begging you, Lord Jesus
Please save my child

Read your Bible each day
And pray for your sins,
This is how all
Of our days should begin

You can pray to yourself
It doesn't have to be out loud,
You're the only One Lord Jesus
That can save my child.

MY BROTHER

He's the apple of my eye
And he's such a great guy,
You would have to pass the test
For he deserves the best

He should be given a crown
'Cause he'll never let you down,
And one other thing
Treat him like a king

He carries himself well
And that we can tell,
He'll always have his youth
That's nothing but the truth

He never raises his voice
And he always keeps his poise,
He's so much like our mother
I'm so thankful he's my brother.

MY PRECIOUS DAUGHTER

A daughter like you
Is one of a kind,
Your beauty and your grace
Is hard to find

You're a precious jewel
And my little queen,
The most precious daughter
That's ever been seen

You spend so much time
Doing things that are pleasing,
While so many others
Are all about teasing

You don't really know
Just how many you bring joy,
Like for the little child
That you gave the Christmas toy

Your talent and your honor
Can never be touched,
When I say that you're my daughter
I get all flushed

Every time I look at you
And the wonderful things you do,
I know you're like no other
And I'm proud to be your mother.

MY WONDERFUL SON

My wonderful son
How great you are,
My very first one
My shiny star

You grew up to be
A very fine man,
Trying hard to see
All that you can

You took your time
To make things right,
Didn't have to spend a dime
To show how bright

You'll go a long way
For you're here to stay,
You're my wonderful son
My very first one.

THE LOVE OF A DAUGHTER

The love of a daughter
Can never be defined,
She loves you unconditionally
That's how she was designed

She watches over you, though you're
Not worthy of all her love and kindness,
She has a special place in her heart
And sees all your faults through blindness

She's filled with warmth and affection
She puts you before herself,
She wants to be there for your protection
And then she takes what's left

She never asks any questions
Of why we can not hire,
She only makes suggestions
That's what her heart desires

The love of a daughter
Cannot be bought in a store,
She has a beauty that comes from within
And lasts forever more!

WHAT I WOULDN'T GIVE

What I wouldn't give
To see my mother's face,
And not feel so alone
Like I'm lost in space,
What I wouldn't give
Just to hear her voice,
And meet in a place
Where we can rejoice

What I wouldn't give
To walk hand in hand,
And travel together
Throughout this land,
What I wouldn't give
To take her out to dinner,
And let everyone know
She's the world's biggest winner

What I wouldn't give
To walk through the door,
And there she would be
Sitting on the floor,
What I wouldn't give
To see her beautiful smile,
And be very proud
Of how she's always in style

There's nothing I wouldn't give
To look her in the eye,
For she'd have been the best mother
No matter how others may try,
There's nothing I wouldn't give
If I could meet my mother,
And she would get to know me,
As well as my sisters and my brother.

YOU'LL ALWAYS HAVE MY TRUST

Every day for me is a test,
Lord knows I've done my best,
To raise all of my children right
I must say it was a bit of a height

I tried to give you
The better things in life,
And I want you to know
I did it without strife

Now there are some things
I have to cover,
That I really hate
I had to discover

You know that you
Can always come to me,
Because standing behind you
I will always be

Loving you
Is a must,
And you will always
Have my trust

We will always
Have respect,
No animosity
Will we ever detect

Because loving my children
Is a very big must,
I want you to know
You will always have my trust.

ReLaTiOnShIpS

ALL THAT YOU CAN

When you've given your man
All the respect that you can,
And he chooses to pay you back
By running the fast track,
When he's checking his beeper
It shows then he's a creeper,
And don't forget the times
He's on the phone,
Always telling you
That he wants to be alone

Make no mistake
He's out in the field,
And using you
Just to be his shield,
What about the nights
He comes in after five?
Trying to sweet talk you
By talking that jive

You try to pretend
You're in a sound sleep,
He can't play with your mind
Because you're too deep,
He wants you to believe
That the problem is you,
He doesn't understand
He's just one in a few

When you know he's screwing you over
Like a four leaf clover,
You've already seen the sign
Now is the time for you to resign.

FREE AT LAST

You hassled and you stalked me
All day long,
When you know darn well
You were in the wrong
You would try calling me
On my cell phone,
And when I didn't answer
You'd call my home

We tried to make it work
But didn't know how,
And walked down the aisle
But were scared to take a vow,
There were so many times
When the phone would ring,
And just to hear your voice
Would make my body sting

To get out of your life
I had to catch the first flight,
And it was at that moment
I had pure delight,
You'd fuss and you'd curse
And wouldn't lower your tone,
But it's okay
Because I've moved on

You need to grow up
And I suggest you not wait,
Get yourself some help
And get your life straight,
Maybe one of these days
This will be part of your past,
But I have to sing and shout
'Cause I'm free at last!

I AM A WOMAN

I am a woman
With lots of integrity,
I am a woman
Who believes in prosperity

I am a woman
Who does not place blame,
I am a woman
Who does not bring shame

I am a woman
With much respect,
I am a woman
That you won't regret

I am a woman
Of deep spirituality,
I am a woman
With congeniality

I am a woman
Who believes in being natural,
I am a woman
Who shies away from disaster

I am a woman
Who holds my family dear,
I am a woman
Who keeps my children near

I am a woman
Of much desire,
I am a woman
That you can admire

I am a woman
Who has never gone astray,
I am a woman
That you can not lay

I am a woman
With much understanding,
I am a woman
That is not too demanding

I am a woman
Who shows my intelligence,
I am a woman
Who will not accept negligence

I am a woman
That has no hate,
I am a woman
That you can't bait

I am a woman
With my own great mind,
I am a woman
Who is one of a kind.

I CAN'T LET GO

You came into my life
And was oh, so sweet,
There was never a cold moment
But so much heat

And here are a few things
I want you to know,
Loving you is good
And I can't let go

You made me feel good
And so excited,
But why bring her
When she's uninvited

Like taking a trip
To the famous Chicago,
Loving you is good
And I can't let go

It would do my heart good
If I knew that you would,
Climb the widest sea
Just to be with me

I'd take the back row
And walk a mile in the snow,
'Cause loving you is good
And I can't let go.

IF YOU COULD READ MY MIND

If you could read my mind
What do you think you'd find?
Would I be given a crown
Or would our worlds come tumbling down?

Would we be committing a crime
Or maybe even doing some time?
Would we be caught in a bind
If you could read my mind?

If you could read my mind
Do you think it'll be so kind?
To show what you'd like to know
Like how our souls can grow

Would we be setting a trap
If I was caught in your lap?
What would you like to find
If you could read my mind?

I'M IN LOVE

I'm in love
With a very fine man,
Who loves me back
And does all that he can

When he gets on his knees
And he makes his pleas,
I thank God above
That I'm In Love

When I go to sleep at night
And I'm all uptight,
I know in the morning
Things will be all right

When I buy me something nice
And he always pays the price,
I'm just like a little dove
For I'm In Love

When I wake up in the morning
And I start my daily journey,
When I look into his eyes
And see he's telling no lies,
I'm like a hand
Stuck in a glove,
Yes, I'm so in love.

IS IT TOO MUCH TO ASK?

Is it too much to ask
For common sense,
Without the relationship
Becoming so tense?

Is it too much to want
To be a beautiful bride,
With such a gorgeous hunk
Standing by my side?

Is it too much to ask
To be the love of your life,
When you've asked me
To be your wife?

Is it too much to ask
For you to spend the day,
And listen to some of the things
That I have to say?

Is it too much to ask
For you to play the part,
Of having love for me
And only me in your heart?

Is it too much to ask
You where you've been,
When you're coming home from work
At a quarter past ten?

Is it too much to ask
You to hold my hand,
Or take a walk on the beach
And play in the sand?

Is it too much to ask
To be by your side,
When you decide to take
Someone else for a ride?

Is it too much to ask
You for a date,
Since I am supposed
To be your mate?

Is it too much to ask
You to treat me nice,
Without you thinking
I'm trying to entice?

Is it too much to ask
You when, where, or why,
Without you getting up
And saying "Good-Bye?"

IT COULD'VE BEEN YOU

I knew this day would come
I discussed it with my mom,
In your heart you knew
It could've been you

You walked away with shame
'Cause you knew you'd played a game,
At that time I had no clue
It could've been you

You said you wanted to marry
No luggage did I carry,
I agree with you too
It could've been you

Other girls were many
I didn't know you had any,
Now you're feeling blue
'Cause it could've been you.

IT IS TIME TO MOVE ON

When the romance is gone
And there is nothing left inside,
It is time for us to move on
So we can gain back our pride,
When the joy turns to pain
As it sometimes do,
Is it worth all the strain?
Or should we find someone new?

When we've gone through the motions
Of trying to do the things that's right,
It is like swimming the widest ocean
Trying hard with all our might,
When the fire has gone out
And sorrow has taken over the joy,
There's no need for us to pout
We must find ourselves another decoy

When we talk on the phone
But can think of nothing much to say,
It is time for us to move on
And we must go our separate way,
When we sit across the aisle
As though we are a total stranger,
We wonder is it worth our while
For now we realize that we are in danger

When we've done the best we could
But the relationship just can't be saved,
That doesn't mean that we're not good
Neither does it mean we've misbehaved,
When we've gone that extra mile
But we've both become withdrawn,
When we can't bring ourselves to smile
We know it is time for us to move on.

I WONDER

I wonder why love
Is such a deadly game?
I had so much to live for
Before you came,
Into my life
With such great talk,
How was I to know
You'd soon take a walk?

It didn't take long
For the love to go sour,
I sit here waiting for you
Hour after hour,
With no where to go
And no one to call,
There's nothing to do
But stare at the wall

I wonder when will
I ever live to be free,
Of all the pain and suffering
That you've caused me?
To say you made a mistake
Would be putting it mild,
Staying out in the streets
And running wild,
Your only excuse
You had the mind of a child

Now that you're gone
I can get my head clear,
Cause one day you'll pay
And the time is getting near,
No matter how long you
Think that you're being sly,
Time will catch up with you
By and by

I wonder what makes a man
Think that he can lie,
'Cause it'll come back on him
Before he die,
So take my advice
And get yourself right,
One of these old days
It'll come to the light

You can hide in the dark
But you'll leave your mark,
It could be little things
Like hearing a dog bark,
So where can you go
And think no one will know,
Can you hide from your lies?
I don't think so
BUT – I WONDER!

I WOULD LIKE TO BELIEVE

I would like to believe
That you are not like any other,
And can give me all I need
So I won't have to look any further,
You have so many of the qualities
That I've been searching for,
You just might have the key
To open up my door

But don't make me any promises
That you know you can not keep,
By playing me for a fool
And making me feel cheap,
This won't be the first time
That my heart has been broken,
Neither will it be the first that
These same words have been spoken

I would like to believe
That you've made up your mind,
And everyone from your past
You've truly put behind,
You came into my life
At just the right time,
You've grown in so many ways
Since we have reached our prime

You made me feel alive again
From the first time that we kissed,
If there's someone else that you're
interested in
Don't put me in the midst,
I would like to believe
That this is something that you want,
But I also have to make sure
That my feelings, you will not taunt.

LET'S FOLLOW OUR HEART

Let us all try
To do our part,
And always remember
To follow our heart,
We sometimes wait
Until it is too late,
Because we're too afraid
Of making a mistake

If we make a mistake
We'll know that we tried,
But let us not fall short
By having too much pride,
When we follow our heart
We might be surprised,
Of how much we have to offer,
So let our heart be our guide

Sometimes when we try
To make a good impression,
We may end up learning
A very hard lesson,
But if we just try
To keep it real,
We'll end up getting
The best out of the deal

So many times we don't
Know how to relate,
Let those be the times
We let our heart dictate,
There is so much good
That we all can do,
And remember that we all
Should have a good heart too.

LET'S MAKE A DEAL

Let's make a deal
To keep our feelings real,
If we decide to go
We'll let each other know

If you just want to play
I will send you on your way,
If you're looking for some fun
I will treat you like a nun

If you think you need a toy
I will treat you like a little boy,
If you're looking for a date
I will treat you like my mate

Let's make a deal
We will try to keep it real,
If you don't treat me nice
You will have to pay the price

Let's make a deal
Tell each other how we feel,
If we become attached
Our feelings should be matched.

LOVE IS

Love is
A very intense affection,
Love is passion which
Needs no detection

Love is to be treated
Only with kindness,
Love is to see ones' mistakes
And weaknesses through blindness

Love is a feeling
Of deep emotion,
Love can only last
With total devotion

To be in love
You must be attracted,
To make love work
You must never be distracted

Love is a feeling that
Should never be neutral,
To be in love your feelings
Must always be mutual

Love isn't meant to be
A game that you can guess,
Love isn't meant to be
A life filled with stress

Love is knowing that
You can always believe,
Love is not being one
That is known to deceive

Love is making promises
That you know you can keep,
Love is not just looking
For a place you can sleep

Love is a feeling that
Is known to inspire,
Love is also a feeling that
Is full of desire

Love is a feeling that
Can become so intense,
Love should never be a feeling
Of false pretense

Love is having the strength
To break old ties,
Love is not coming into a relationship
Filled with lies

Love is being with someone
That you can adore,
Love is knowing that you no longer
Have a need to explore.

LOVE IS JUST A FAIRY TALE

You always love to boast
And that's what makes it gross,
You met your man in jail
Love is just a fairy tale

He made you act the fool
So you went and quit your school,
He put your house for sale
Love is just a fairy tale

You let him have his way
No bills he had to pay,
We all wish you well
Love is just a fairy tale

He took you for a ride
With the things he had to hide,
Although he is a male
Love is just a fairy tale

You took him to meet your mom
Though he acted very calm,
She knew you were going through hell
Love is just a fairy tale.

LOVE IS LIKE A FLOWER

Love is like a flower
It needs nourishing every hour,
If you squeeze it much too tight
It will wither during the night

If you leave it in the dark
It'll dry up and feel like bark,
If you handle it with great care
It will strengthen up and bare

If you throw out too many seeds
It will look like a bunch of weeds,
If you treasure it and admire
It will grow to your desire.

LOVE IS NOT A GAME WE PLAY

Love is not a game we play
Just because we can't have our way,
When you find that special one
Try very hard to build a bond

Be true to your mate from day to day
And be careful about the things you say,
We must learn to appreciate
All the little things we get from our mate

You must think twice before you lay
And remember that we can't always do as we may,
If you choose to be a fool
Blame yourself for not being cool

There are times when we don't do as we are told
And we may be asked to hit the road,
But when we break that golden rule
We may be erased from their schedule

In order to make love a real success
We must do all that we can and give it our best,
Though some may see it as a time delay
Love is not a game we play.

MY BABY'S FATHER

You're a cat in a hat
And a darn disgrace,
An embarrassment to all
The men in our race

You ran out our baby's life
When he was just a child,
All you wanted to do
Was be free and wild

You never took the time
To teach him how to play,
And never heard a word
That he would soon say

You'll never know the joy
Of what we had together,
Now he's all grown up
You want him to buy you leather

You never went a day
To check out his school,
But I can truly tell you
He's nobody's fool

He can teach you a thing or two
In Technology,
Though he graduated with honors
In Psychology

You had nothing to offer
And I don't know the reason why
I didn't come to my senses
And see right through your lie

He's the best thing that could've happened
and I appreciate,
All the things we do together
And when we meditate

He always takes the time
To say, "Mama, I Love You,
And when you see my father
Tell him I love him too"

Though you missed your opportunity
It doesn't seem to bother,
I'll be forever sorry
That you're my baby's father.

MY FRIEND, MY LOVER

I woke up one night
And to my surprise,
There was the man of my dreams
In a fancy disguise,
We began to communicate
Before long we had a date,
He was like no other
My friend, my lover

We'd sit and we'd chat
And play a game or two,
We enjoyed doing that
And we called each other boo,
He should have himself cloned
And put one in every zone,
This man could be your brother,
But he's my friend, my lover

We'd stare in each other's eyes
We'd give each other that look,
As though we'd won a prize
That was all that it took,
If you fail to recognize
Or just don't realize,
You'd think he's undercover
My friend, my lover

He pulled me to the side
And said baby, I love you,
He gave me a brand new ride
And said it's long overdue,
No one can ever measure
Nor fill me with such pleasure,
I truly thank his mother
For my friend, my lover.

MY LOVE IS STONE COLD

My love for you has gone stone cold
The lies you tell are so very old,
You didn't appreciate
The good thing that you had,
Until it was too late
And things had gotten bad

If you look around
And search through your soul,
You might realize
You were playing the wrong role

You could've treated me right
And things would've been well,
But all of your lies
Just would not sell

When I look at you
I try not to believe,
That I am the one
You chose to deceive

Now as I look back
I guess I wanted to explore,
With no idea
Of what you had in store

It is hard to accept
The things you put me through,
Or what I gave up
Just to be with you

But deep inside
I know you'll regret this day,
After hearing everything
That I have to say

I went out of my way
To keep from letting you go,
But in the end
It was you who made it so

When you did your thing
You were so bold,
Now it is too late
Because my love is stone cold.

MY MIND IS TOO DEEP

Deep inside there is so much pain
And so many things I need you to explain,
How we made it this far and had to turn back
Because of the joy and the feelings that we lack

Deep down low I feel I must go
We can not stay together just for show,
When I fall in love again it will be on my term
And the next lucky guy will have to confirm

When I'm looking for someone I'll send out an application
And go through each one with total dedication,
The thoughts that run through my mind go so very deep
You will need to be a prince instead of some creep

There won't be a need for you to apply
I'll need someone in which I can rely,
There'll be no more times when I'll sit and weep
This I won't settle for, because my mind is too deep.

NO COMING BACK

I see the light in your eyes
But we must break the ties,
There is no coming back
I caught you in the sack

You said you'd be true to me
Like I was true to you,
But from these tears we can see
You broke my heart in two

Just the other day
When you thought you were alone,
I was in my room
Listening on the phone

You said "Baby just hold tight
I'm on my way,"
So I dropped the phone,
Didn't know what to say

Now I'm through with you
For you can never be true,
It's not worth the time
You leave me sad and blue

So pick up all your stuff
I have it on the floor,
The only thing left now
Is for you to walk out that door

So ladies listen up
Take note of what I have to say,
Don't ever let your man
Treat you this way

No matter what you do
Each and every day,
While you're falling in love
He's only out to play

Yesterday it was I
Today it is me,
What the hell ever happened
To the word called we?

You made your bed hard
Now you have to lay,
Hello and good-bye
Is all I have to say

This is not the time
To try and make a come-back,
'Cause remember my love
I caught you in the sack,
And baby, there is no coming back!

NOW AIN'T THE TIME

Now ain't the time
For me and you,
To walk down the aisle
And say Yes, I do

You're over there
And I'm over here,
My feelings have been dying
All throughout the year

Love is an obstacle
A thorn in your heart,
That's just one of the things
Keeping us apart,
Now all of a sudden
You're ready to start,
Now ain't the time.

Love to you
Is like a merry go round,
But the pain in my heart
Is keeping me bound

One day you're here to stay
The next day you're on your way,
There are so many things
That I'd like to say,
But now ain't the time.

I look in the mirror
And what do I see,
Just a hollow, hollow
Shadow staring at me,

With tears in my eyes
And the pain on my face,
I think Lord, have mercy
Oh, what a disgrace,
There are so many others
Waiting for your place,
And now that you'd like
To get back in the race,
Now ain't the time

I'm a very small girl
With a very big mind,
And I need me a man
That's one of a kind,
You had your chance
But you chose to dance,
All over the place
With no romance,
When just the other day
You gave me a glance,
But now ain't the time

Now ain't the time
To be sad and blue,
Just sitting in my bedroom
Thinking of you,
There are so many things
I'm ready to do,
The next time you find love
I hope you'll be true,
But there's one thing left
I need to say to you,
Now ain't the time

When I lay in my bed
And I think of you,
I remember the times
I could've played the games too

But loving you, I thought
Was meant to be true,
Little did I know
I'd be sad and blue
If you want to know the answer
Of getting back with you,
Now ain't the time.

NOW THAT YOU ARE GONE

Now that you are gone
I truly feel alone,
Our love was so intact
I thought for sure you'd take me back

Now that you are gone
I see the things that I did wrong,
You thought you'd been a fool
I thought you were really cool

Now that you are gone
I've decided to change my tone,
Since we had made a pact
I thought our love was a fact

Now that you are gone
It hurts me to the bone,
If I had done things right
I'd have you every night.

ONCE IN A WHILE

Once in a while
When you meet a nice guy,
As you're sitting on the beach
Watching passers-by

It runs through your mind
Why can't we elope?
It's like looking at him
Through a telescope

You remember back to the time
Of a passage you read,
He's thinking the same thing
Only he hasn't said

Once in a while
When your mind goes free,
And you're holding hands
Sitting under a tree

You begin to think about
Yours and his future,
Now you have to hope
That the feeling is mutual

You jump to your feet
And begin to smell the roses,
And right at that moment
He gets down and proposes

Once in a while
When you're in denial,
You think, what's wrong with me
This man is a liar

Don't blame yourself
Because you're a human being,
Just take this moment
To feel like a queen

There's nothing wrong with dreaming
And wearing a big smile,
As long as you do it
Just once in a while.

ONLY YOU CAN MAKE THIS DREAM COME TRUE

There are so many things
I wish I could see,
And so many other places
That I know I could be,
But there is nothing more
I'd like to do,
Than to take this opportunity
To spend time with you

There are so many things
I want to say,
But for some odd reason
I can't find the way,
So I will have to write
It all down on paper,
And you can enjoy reading
It sometime later

There are so many songs
I'd like to hear you sing,
As you present to me
A big diamond ring,
But only you can make
This dream come true,
For there is no other place
I'd rather be than here with you

There are so many things
That I can do very well,
But at this time it is
Hard for me to tell,
I can say for sure
That my feelings are true,
And I would like to spend
The rest of my life with you.

ROLL IN THE HAY

Like a bird in a cage
You have so much rage,
You're like a time clock
With every girl on the block

When I look into the glass
What I see is first class,
So it doesn't really pay
To have a roll in the hay

You can satisfy your urge
But you better not splurge,
You can ride on a bike
Or you can take a hike

Just remember to be sure
Of the things you endure,
And the price you have to pay
To take a roll in the hay

We must go our separate ways
In just a matter of days,
'Cause try as we might
We're destined to fight

When you held me tight
We could've made this thing right,
But it's too late in the day
For just a roll in the hay.

SO MANY TIMES

There were so many times
That I wanted to give up,
But I knew what I had to do
My tears were enough to fill a cup,
And it was all because of you

I had to pick up the pieces
And go on with my life,
For every day the pain decreases
But at first it cuts like a knife

I'm on my way to full recovery
For that was only a test,
I thank you for that discovery
Now I can take care of the rest

There were many times I had to guess
Was it me that made such a mess?
I know now that I can go on
For my troubles have already gone.

THERE ARE NO MORE TEARS TO SHED

There are no more tears
For me to shed,
For I have cried them
All out in bed

Late at night when you
Go out to creep,
I cry in my pillow
Until I fall asleep

Many days would go by
When I'd sit and cry,
For you were very good
At telling a big lie

My life has been sad
Since the day we wed,
But there are no more tears
For me to shed

Nights would come
And nights would go,
The lies would also
Come straight in a row

I couldn't believe
A thing you said,
So there are no more tears
For me to shed

We did not get along
And we had no fun,
Each day after work
You were on the run

I cried so much I felt
As though I was dead,
Now there are no more tears
For me to shed

People would always try to tell me
Bad things about you,
Some I didn't believe,
Others I knew were true

Now you can't believe
The life you've led,
But there are no more tears
For me to shed.

THERE WAS A TIME

There was a time when you
Could trust your best friend,
And be there for each other
Until the very end

Now those times
Have come and gone,
And our best friends
Have since moved on

If I had a problem
You made it your problem too,
And you knew that I
Would always be there for you

Now we realize
It was false pretense,
We're no longer there
For each other's defense

When we got sick
We felt each other's pain,
We'd stay with each other
If it meant standing in the rain

Now there are some things
We didn't know about each other,
For those were the things
We kept hidden undercover

When we shared our secrets
We were the only ones that knew,
We felt in order to be friends
We would have to be true

But times have changed
And we're no longer there,
And now our secrets
Are known everywhere

There was a time when you
Could have been my twin,
This is how most
Friendships begin

But in the end we'd
Betray each other's trust,
Now this friendship
Has been turned to dust.

THE TWO OF US

The two of us were meant to be
So many beautiful times had we,
We made the best of every hour
And hoped our love would never go sour

The two of us would dance all night
And eat our dinner by candlelight,
And when we stopped to take a break,
We'd hold each other until we wake

The two of us had so many things
Like Cadillacs and diamond rings,
But even those were not enough
To keep this relationship
from ending so rough

The two of us traveled far and near
We did these things throughout the year,
But now it's time to sever our ties
For there is no way to get past the lies

The two of us would keep our dates
With many agenda on our plates,
But as we know good things must end
There's some other business I must attend.

THIS HEART'S FOR YOU

Just in case that
You have no clue
I'd like you to know
This heart's for you
This is no lie
This is no line
I want you to be
My Valentine

You are so cute
You are so fine
Will you be
My Valentine
I'll take you to a movie
I'll take you out to dine
If you will be
My Valentine

Rain or shine
I'll make you mine
I want you to be
My Valentine
Today is not the day
For us to fall apart
Let's get together
And connect this heart.
Be my Valentine

Be very smart
And give me your heart.
Let me be your Valentine
Now is not the time
For us to depart
Please find a way
To let me back into your heart.
I want to be your Valentine

TOO HARD TO BEAR

There are so many things that I could say
About the times we spent with each other,
But I'm sure if you could have it your way
You'd keep it all undercover

You can get upset or you can put it to rest
I leave that all up to you,
But I want everyone to know I did my best
There was nothing else that I could do

You said you wanted to have your space
And you asked me to understand,
But I would never know my place
For you traveled throughout the land

You had a woman over there and a few over here
And that became too hard to bear,
So I got to the place I didn't want you near
Because I could no longer care!

YOU ARE MY DESTINY

No matter where I go
Or who I may see,
You are the only man
That was ever meant to be,
A part of my life
Which only I can define,
I'm waiting for the day
We let our love begin to shine

You are my destiny
I wouldn't have it any other way,
Just carrying you in my heart
Helps me get through the day,
Now I'm not insane
This is rationality,
I want everyone to know
That you are my destiny.

YOU MUST TAKE A CHANCE

You must take a chance
On true romance,
Or you won't know what to do
When it finds you

You may never know
How much love can grow,
If you decide to give up
For there is no measuring cup

You might find love in your school
Or maybe at the swimming pool,
And you may miss out on a great dance
If you don't take a chance

You must make yourself look nice
And you might sometimes have to entice,
But you may never find romance
If you don't take a chance

You could miss out on the best
Because you've given up on all the rest,
If you don't find reason to believe
True romance you may never receive

You can ride in the nicest cars
Or drink at the finest bars,
But in order to find romance
You must take a chance

Just because you have a pretty face
Does not always keep you in the race,
The only way to find romance
Is you must take a chance.

YOU'RE MY BOO

You're my boo
And I love you too,
I spend most of my time
Thinking of you,
We've come a long way
And have a long way to go,
You're always here
When I'm feeling low

You show me a good time
Each and every day,
I hope there's never a time
You won't treat me this way,
We glide and we slide
On the dance floor,
I'm beginning to feel you
More and more

When we go out together
Even in bad weather,
I'm floating on air
Just like a feather,
You take me out to dinner
And you pull out my chair,
And going back to the car
You run your fingers through my hair

You're like a night in shiny armor
Who rescued me,
And have my eyes wide open
As far as I can see,
We're made for each other
And that's so true,
I love you
Because you're my Boo.

Spiritual

DID YOU REMEMBER

Did you remember to thank the Lord today
For all the blessings He's given you?
And never once did He ask you to pay
For making them all come true

Did you remember to get on your knees and pray
When you went to bed last night?
What was the last thing you heard Him say
When you went to turn out the light?

Did you remember to testify
About the joy His love brings?
By doing all you can to rectify
And making peace of petty things

Did you remember to wish others well
Or help out someone in need?
That would be a way for Him to tell
That you have done a very good deed

Did you remember to follow His advice
And do only the things that are right?
Like doing your best to treat everyone nice
And loving Him with all your might.

FIRST AND FOREMOST IN MY LIFE

I always put Jesus
First and foremost in my life,
For if I don't, I know
I will have to pay the price

There are so many times when
Other people may turn away,
But in my heart, I know
His love is here to stay

I love my children, and
I know they love me too,
But nobody else can love me,
The way that Jesus do

Jesus has a love
That is so divine,
It is like no other love
That we can define

When I am sick,
I know His love can heal,
And I always give Him blessings
Before eating every meal

I never feel alone
For He is always around,
He comes into my life
Without ever making a sound

When I need Jesus, I know
He'll let His blessings flow,
He is always with me
Even when I'm feeling low

He was born to the Virgin Mary
And in a manger He lay,
His friends betrayed His trust
In each and every way

He was beat on the cross
And there He was left to die,
But He gave His life
To save you and I

Some think in order to get to Heaven
We need only to be a good wife,
But I will always keep Jesus
First and foremost in my life.

FREEDOM FOR ALL

God gave us the right to speak
And the right to make a phone call,
Love between races have always been weak
We've got to do something to break this wall

To burn a cross in someone else's yard
Is only a cry for help,
But when we choose not to do our part
We've ignored the hand that we were dealt

Because I am black and you are white
We should all be treated the same,
It does not mean that I am wrong and you are right,
Neither does it give you the right to call me out my name

Freedom was not meant to be for one
And not for another,
For when it is all said and done
I am your sister and you are my brother

We must all fight for what we know is right
In order to do what the Bible said,
Get on our knees and pray day and night
And remember the things that we have read

God does not approve of the way we live
When we choose not to obey His command,
Each of us must learn to love and forgive
For He made this a demand

Like Johnnie Cochran said in court one day
When a young black woman was turned away,
If you design or build a mall
It must be open to one and all.

114

GOD IS JUST

God is just
In all that He do,
He created us both
Me and you,
He won't let us down
And He'll never turn His back,
He'll take care of us
In all that we lack

God is just
And in Him I trust,
One day our bodies
Will return to dust,
I want to be ready
When He calls my name,
I try to live right
Because this is no game

God is just
And on Him I rely,
I'm going home to join Him
By and by,
If you want to go to Heaven
You know what you must do,
When those trumpets sound
I want to hear my name too

God is just
To love Him is a must,
To have your pot of gold
Will only turn to rust,
Sex before marriage
That's only lust,
I love God
Because God is just.

GOD IS NOT PLEASED

One day as I sat in front of the TV
I could not believe what I saw starring back at me,
So many of my people were fighting for their lives
Men, women and children and so many young wives

They were hanging from trees and on top of roof tops
But all we heard in the media was criticism from the cops,
Our people were begging and trying to defeat death
But for so many of them, they would take their last breath

I still can't comprehend just how badly my
people were being treated
But what I do know is that their lives had been cheated,
Our leaders didn't try to make them feel any more at ease
And for that we can be assured that God is not pleased

Hurricane Katrina is what they called her by name
But Katrina is not what brought this nation to shame,
It was our Congress men and women, and the media too
And the things they had to say, most of which were not true

They would make up things just to make their ratings higher
But who cares about ratings, when we know that they're a liar,
My people were being treated as if no one had any care
And every moment that I saw them, it was too hard for me to bear

As a nation, we can never offer a big enough apology
With the harm that has been put forth with such
disgraceful ideology,
You might think that you are better than these very ones
But always remember that these are God's
daughters and sons

116

They would wade through water just to get to the better side
Where they knew that help would come and where they would try
to catch a ride,
Not knowing where they would go or what they would do
Just hoping for some kindness from the likes of me and you

We can only imagine what was going through their mind
If you couldn't see their frustration, you would've had to be blind,
There's no other summation that one can concede
For I truly have to believe that God is not pleased

Night after night and day after day
These people were being treated in such an ungodly way,
With no food to eat nor water to drink,
Just the very sight of it all would make my heart begin to sink.

There is so much more that we all could have done
But some of us thought that the whole ordeal was fun,
People are human, no matter where they may come from
Their home is their livelihood, though they may live in a slum

There is still so much hatred because of the color of our skin
But we must all stand together, if one day we plan to win,
We can only be defeated, if we give up and do not fight
We can also become winners, if we remember to do what is right

When we see children dying and old people wasting away
"They were stealing and looting", is this all that we can say?
Even in such a disaster, some saw the need to tease
But only a true Christian would know that God is not pleased.

GOD PROMISED

God promised He'd keep us near
He'd give us comfort when we shed a tear,
He'd save His children both young and old
He has a love that's like pure gold

God promised that He would come back
And no necessities would we lack,
He'd be with us whether we're
awake or asleep
And all of our souls He would surely keep

God promised He would not forsake
And He has never made a mistake,
He sits up high and looks down low
He'd always be with us wherever we go

God promised He'd save our souls
He'd ease our burdens and our heavy loads,
He would not put more on us than we could bear
And He'd always make our enemies rare

God promised He would not lie
He would be with us even when we die,
He lets us know He's in control
And no one else can take His role.

I AM GOING TO A BETTER RESTING PLACE

When my body gets frail and I lay down to die
Please don't be sad, nor weep, nor cry,
I have done my best to win this race
Now I am going to a better resting place

Think of the good times that is yet to come
For there are so many more, and more, and then some,
It may not be right now, or so it may seem
But think of this as being just a dream

This is the time for us all to rejoice
Knowing how good it is to hear our Savior's voice,
Remember when Jesus died upon the cross
And don't think of me as being a loss

When you go to bed and try to fall asleep
Please promise me that you will not weep,
I will still be with you every day
And I hope that you will continue to pray

God said that one day our bodies would return to dust
Now you must turn to Him and put all your trust,
This is not the time for you to be sad
For I have been true to Him, and now I am glad

I already knew that my time was near
And I want you all to know that I have no fear,
On this earth, I have given so much love
Now it is time for me to join my Savior above

If I go to bed and not wake up tonight
Be thankful that I have no more battles to fight,
I will always remember your smiling face
But now I am going to a better resting place.

I BELIEVE IN JESUS

When I've searched and I've read
And all is done and said,
I don't try to deceive us
For I believe in Jesus

When I've told myself no matter
Things will only make me sadder,
I do the things that'll please us
Cause I believe in Jesus

When you have too much at stake
And now you must forsake,
We don't know where that'll lead us
So I believe in Jesus.

I CAN ALWAYS TURN TO JESUS

I can always turn to Jesus
Because I know He will prevail,
I know that He will be with me
When everything else seems to fail

I know when I need His love
I will never be denied,
And His love will always protect me
For it can never be defied

There are times when so many of us
Cannot resist temptation,
But I've always turned to my Savior,
Since the day of my creation

I will always make sure to stay
In my Savior's corner,
And do nothing but praise Him
And give Him the honor

When you decide to persecute me
For the wrong things that I oppose,
I can always turn to Jesus
For it is these wrong things we should dispose

I know He'll never forsake me
Nor will He do anything wrong,
So I turn to Him for comfort
Because I know that's where I belong.

I DON'T CARE WHAT NOBODY SAYS

I don't care what
Nobody says,
I love my Lord more
And more each day

I live for His blessings
And to glorify His name,
For if I choose to disobey Him
I have only myself to blame

I can't live a lie
And pretend that I don't know,
For the truth is in His word
And to Him my soul I owe

I always take a stand
When I know He's being deceived,
And believe I've done the right thing
Because my heart feels relieved

Others may not appreciate
Or just don't know the sacrifice,
In my heart I can not hate
I just learn to treat everyone nice

Jesus promised me a life free from sin
As long as His name I proclaim,
I'll obey His word and follow His command
For Heaven is my aim

If we don't believe
That He is coming again,
Then all of our prayers
Will be done in vain.

I FORESEE A BETTER TOMORROW

I foresee a
Better tomorrow,
And all of the great things
That will follow

When our black youth
Won't be thrown in jail,
While other non-blacks
Will be allowed to make bail

When we won't be forced
To give up our crown,
Because others feel
Our skin is too brown

When I speak to you and
You won't turn your head,
Instead of acknowledging me back
You pretend you hadn't heard

When our wonderful children
Won't be denied,
But their strengths and talents
Will be recognized

When black and white
Can be a pair,
Without anyone having
To point and stare

When you won't think of us
As committing a crime,
Just because we ask
If you knew the time

When we'll have the right
To be as bold as you,
And you'll get to know
There is good in us too

When we can build our
Homes next to yours,
Without crosses being burned
Or signs on our doors

When we can walk into a store
Without being arrested,
Or feeling like our rights
Are always being tested

When our young boys
Can stop taking the blame,
Just so you can protect
Someone else's name

When our students will get credit
For passing the test,
Knowing that they did better
Than all the rest

When you will be able
To accept the fact,
There is nothing wrong
With us being black

When you will stop
Pretending to be blind,
Always thinking that we
Should be left behind

When we can all get together
And celebrate,
Without you feeling you must
Be there to delegate

When we'll be able to show
That we do have pride,
Then all of this hatred
Will have to subside

When you'll see us like
You see other man-kind,
And realize that you can't
Destroy our mind

When our children won't have
To grow up in sorrow,
I want you to know
I foresee a better tomorrow.

I KNOW OF A HOME

I know of a home far from here
Where angels sing and life is dear,
Where there is no cold or winter snow
This is the home where I want to go

Where everyone there is filled with joy
And there is nothing that we can destroy,
Where we won't do things just for show
This is the home where I'm trying to go

Where only those who followed His command
Will know where it is and will understand,
Where everyone's hearts are full of glow
This is the home where we all should go

I know of a home far from here
Where things are the same throughout the year,
Where God sits up high and looks down low
This is the home where I'm going to go.

I'LL BE WAITING AT GOD'S GATE

We always have our reasons
For doing the things we do,
Like God made different seasons
He made us different too

Our skin may be different colors
But our blood is all the same,
We should treat each other like brothers
And believe in Jesus name

We may live in different places
But we put our trust in Him,
Though we come from different races
Our faith should never be dim

We can always be polite
And treat each other nice,
By showing us just how bright
And knowing that will suffice

Your hair may be long and straight
Mine may look just like wool,
While I'll be waiting at God's gate
You'll be wishing that you could.

I LOVE YOU LORD

I love you Lord
For all that you do,
And depend on you
My whole life through

I say my prayers
At night before bed,
And have faith in you
Because I know that you are not dead

I love you Lord
In every respect,
You saved my soul
And I'll never forget

When I leave this world
I want to be in your glory,
I'm not saying these things
Just to make a good story

I love you Lord
And I praise your name,
I'll spread your word
So others may do the same

I obey your gospel
Because I know it is true,
Unlike some of us
Who have no clue

I love you Lord
Because that was your plan,
For us to be saved
We must do all that we can

I love you Lord
For you are true,
I can count on you
When I'm feeling blue

I love your Lord
With all my might,
For you are pleasing
In God's sight

I love you Lord
Without a doubt,
All of your praises
I'll sing and shout!

I NEED YOU LORD

I need you Lord to save my soul
To see that my life takes on a better role,
To give me strength to overcome my fears
And keep the faith throughout my years

I need you Lord to have mercy on me
To open my eyes and make me see,
We all will have some rainy days
But we must lean on you in so many ways

I need you Lord to hold my hand
To walk with me while I'm on this land,
I need you Lord to be by my side
And cleanse my soul so I will abide

I need you Lord to be my guide
To be the one for me to confide,
I need you Lord to fulfill my dream,
I know in order to get to heaven
I must join your team.

I WANT TO BE READY

There'll come a time
For you to make up your mind,
If you want to go to Heaven
Or be left behind

God said He'd love us
And He'd never forsake,
In His great Kingdom
I want to partake

I want to be ready
When He calls my name,
And I hope and I pray
That you'll do the same

It's only a matter of time
Before Judgment Day,
And for all of our sins
He will make us pay

I do my best
To try to live my life right,
And do only the things
That are pleasing in His sight

I'm ready to enter
His pearly white gate,
To live a life of sin
Would be a mistake.

JUST LET ME ENJOY THIS PEACE

Life on earth hasn't been so dear
No more harsh words will I ever have to hear,
All of my pain has now been ceased
Just let me enjoy this peace,
I've waited so long to be with my Lord
I'm now in a place where I will get my reward,
Love each other and your blessings will increase
Just let me enjoy this peace

There will be no ridicule up in heaven
Something I've lived with since I was about seven,
This time I didn't have to sign any lease
Just let me enjoy this peace,
God called my name and I had to obey
We all must take this journey one day,
There's not a better place that I'd rather be
Just let me enjoy this peace

I'm happy with where I am today
I made sure to stay obedient to God and pray,
We'll sit at the table and partake in our feast
Just let me enjoy this peace,
Remember to thank God for the time that we shared
I pray for you to know that I really cared,
Now God wants me to let go and release
Just let me enjoy this peace

So many times we try so hard to hold on
I knew I would be ready when He called me home,
All disappointments and sorrow can now cease
Just let me enjoy this peace,
Be thinking of me while I'm away
And keep God in your lives each and every day,
But don't think of me as being deceased
Just let me enjoy this peace.

LEAVE EVERYTHING TO GOD

When things get too complicated
We should put them in God's hands,
For all these things He created
And we know just where He stands

We may sometimes feel discouraged
When things are not going right,
But there is a way to be encouraged
By praying every night

We can't always be right
Sometimes we all do wrong,
Our sins will come to light
For God sits on His throne

When you've done your best to fix it
Just like a lightning rod,
It's time that you admitted
You'll leave everything to God.

LET US ALL MAKE A DIFFERENCE

Let us all make a difference
In someone else's life,
It could be a total stranger
Or it could be your ex-wife,
When we see someone in need
Let us lend a helping hand,
Let us try to make a difference
All throughout the land

When we're on our daily journey
And we see someone is stranded,
Let us stop and lend our service
Even though it is not demanded,
When we get on our knees and pray
And ask the Lord for His deliverance,
We can also remember to thank Him
For letting us make a difference

Let us forget about being selfish
And think of someone else,
And remember all the times
When we needed help ourselves,
It won't take very long
Though it may not be in the plan,
When we see someone in need
We should all take a stand

Every evening after work
When we watch the daily news,
There's a lot that we can learn
For it shows us so many clues,
Let us all make a difference
In someone else's life,
For the Lord will give us our blessings
For doing something nice.

LORD, PLEASE FORGIVE ME

Lord, please forgive me
For everything that I have done,
And cleanse me of my wicked ways
So I'll be able to move on

Forgive me for not doing the things
That is pleasing in your sight,
And give me the strength to be able
To do only the things that are right

Lord, forgive me for everything I've said
That may not always have been true,
And help me to do only the things
That truly pleases you

Forgive me for any resentment
That may be built up in my heart,
And please strengthen my soul
So I'll always do my part

Lord, please forgive me
If I fail to obey,
And help me to understand
In each and every way

Forgive me for being disobedient
And for making the wrong choice,
And please be there to correct me
If I should lose my voice

Lord, please forgive me
For not always listening to your word,
Help me to put behind me
All the wrong things that I have heard

Forgive me for not appreciating
All the little things that you do,
And show me how I can live
So I'll always be true to you

Lord, please forgive me
For all my sinful ways,
And help me to overcome my iniquities
For the rest of my days

Forgive me for my mistakes
And for any jealousy that I may have shown,
And help me to find a way
To make Your spirit known.

Amen

LORD, WHY ME?

I've always been one to do
What I could to help another,
With no appreciation from anyone
Except sometimes my only brother,
I often wonder just what it could be
So all I can say is Lord, why me?

You'd think I would be treated nice
Because I'm always giving praise,
Not looking down on others
Though they may have their crooked ways,
If you took the time to know me
Then you could very well see,
Now all I can say is Lord, why me?

Because I wasn't like you
I didn't belong in your click,
Or maybe it was because I wasn't strong
Enough to keep from getting sick,
Adam and Eve weren't perfect
And neither are we,
But all I can say is Lord, why me?

One of these days you will
Know just who was true,
It was not the ones
With the worldly things like you,
I'm alright with You, God
And I put my trust in Thee,
And no longer do I have to ask
Lord, why me?

MY TALK WITH JESUS

Jesus came into
My life one day,
And here are some of the words
He had to say

"Wake up my child
And get on your knees,
I am your Savior
And I hear your pleas"

I thought at first
It was only a dream,
It was so unreal
Or so it would seem

I crawled out of bed
And got on the floor,
I looked toward Heaven and cried,
Please tell me more

He said, "I know everything
That you have been through,
And I also know
That your heart is true

But there's so much more
That you deserve,
Don't let life throw
You another curve"

"To get into My Kingdom
You must obey,
There is no more time
For you to delay

You must go to church
With the rest of my flock,
'Cause time is running out
On your clock."
I said, "Lord I want
My soul to be right,
I also want
My burdens light

And please cleanse me
Of all my sin,
It is your grace
I want to win

Lord, you know I give
You all the praise,
And I'll love and cherish you
All of my days

When I get to Heaven
And have no more miles to run,
I want to hear Him say,
'That was a job well done.'"

MY TESTIMONY

I was once considered a beautiful lady
But now I look like a monster,
I had lots of dreams from the time I was a baby
So many things I wanted to conquer

I won't let this disease cause me to lose faith
Because God will always have the last say,
Neither will I let my beliefs go to waste
For He has His reasons for making me this way

I struggled from time to time with many sick days
But prayed for the strength not to lose any hope,
God showed me different things in so many ways
But sometimes I felt I was at the end of my rope

Though I've been through many trials
And tribulations in my life,
This is a testimony that I must tell
There were times it caused me
Not to be a good wife,
But I know that God has the power
To make me well

Because I may not look the same as before
I have a beauty that comes from within,
And I've learned that
The things I should adore,
Are not always
The things I had to begin.

NOTHING IN LIFE IS A GUARANTEE

We get up and go to work each and every day
To get the things we need to live and bills to pay,
We live in a world where almost nothing is free
For nothing in life is a guarantee

No one promised that we wouldn't have to strive
To get what we need just to stay alive,
We try to be as happy as we can be
But nothing in life is a guarantee

When we go to sleep, we don't know if we'll awake
So let's be sure and give God our soul to take,
We know that He is our only key
And nothing in life is a guarantee

Jesus' word has always been good
And His word is where I have always stood,
He said He would be back to save you and me
He is the only one that can make any guarantee.

ONE DAY MY TROUBLES WILL BE OVER

One day my troubles will all be over
There will be no more need for me to cry,
For when my Savior calls me home to Glory
I will just bow my head and die

So many times I have sat and wondered
Of how my life would come to an end,
But life on earth is filled with so much thunder
I'm just waiting for my Lord to descend

There'll be no more need for me to feel lonely
Nor will there be a need for any more pain,
For Jesus is the friend that I have only
And my life will be rid of any more strain

There are days my life is like a pillar of cloud
Never was it like a four leaf clover,
But now I am happy and very proud
For one day my troubles will all be over.

PRAYER IS THE ANSWER

When you look into the sky
And ask Dear Lord, why?
When you're having a bad day
And you don't know what to say,
There's only one way
Get on your knees and pray,
Prayer is the answer.

Late at night when you
Turn out the light,
And you think everyone
Is out of sight,
Don't feel sad to be alone
'Cause I'm here to tell you
That's so wrong,
God is just like a beautiful sun ray
Shining brightly through your way,
Don't give up on life today
All you need to do is pray,
Prayer is the answer.

When you wake up in the morning
And begin to take your shower,
Give God the Glory
'Cause He has the power,
He'll show you the way
Just bow your head and pray,
Prayer is the answer.

When time goes by
And you feel you need to cry,
And you want to be alone
'Cause you feel you might die,
Don't wait another day
Turn to God and pray,
Prayer is the answer.

STRIVING FOR THAT SPIRITUAL BEING

There is so much more to life than just the
human being.
We should all be doing God's
Work so that one day we'll
be able to experience
having some of that
Spiritual Being.
Following His advice, and
Doing everything that we
can to treat each other nice.

Not just the ones that
We think live up to our
standard. If we're not careful,
These could be the very ones
Who have made sure that God's
Words have been slandered.

We can't go to Church
And believe that God is pleased.
Then come home afterwards
doing things that will bring
shame to His name.
There is so much more we need
to do so He may be appeased.

We must eat right,
live right, sing right,
love right, pray right.
To get into God's Kingdom,
Everything we do
must be right in the eyes
of the Lord. We must do
all of these things both
day and night.

We cannot get to Heaven
Just by talking the talk.
Words are cheap and
can always be misconstrued.
These words must be turned
into actions. He will know
we've obeyed His command
when He see us walking the walk.
God is no fool, and try as we might,
we can never fool God. Only those
of us who have obeyed His word and
followed His command will be
able to enter into His great Kingdom.
That is why we must all
be striving for that
Spiritual Being.

God bless each and every one of
you for your kind words and thoughts
of consideration that you've shown me
while writing this publication. It truly has
been a blessing that I have been able to
communicate with all of you. Continue to
keep me and my family in your prayers each and
every day as we will keep you in our prayers
as well. Thank you very much.

THE POWER OF PRAYER

When you wake from a dream
Or your worst nightmare,
Always remember
The power of prayer

When you can't understand
Or you think no one cares,
Always remember
The power of prayer

If you think you can't deliver
Or is scared to take a dare,
Always remember
The power of prayer

If things seem to devour
Hour after hour,
Always remember
The power of prayer

When you want to give up
And not accept the communion cup,
Always remember
The power of prayer

If you're scared to take the test
Because you think you know what's best,
Always remember
The power of prayer

When you're thinking to yourself
I'll put my heart up on a shelf,
Always remember
The power of prayer

If you haven't read your Bible
And you hold yourself liable,
Always remember
The power of prayer.

WHY MUST WE OBEY THE GOSPEL?

Why must we obey the Gospel
And do what the Lord says?
Because it'll make us better people
And cleanse us of our ungodly ways

Why don't we know the difference
Between living in His Word and living in sin?
Because some of us think that we're immortal
While others just can't seem to comprehend

Why won't we all just believe in Him
After all His books that we have read?
Because not all of us will make it to Heaven,
That's what the Bible said

Why can't we take His word
And get it through our head?
By the time this world becomes a perfect place
We'll probably all be dead.

YOU MUST HOLD ON

My life is full of pain
And filled with drops of rain,
Jesus said, "You're not alone,
Just hold on"

I take my meds in bed
Did what the doctors said,
Jesus whispered in a tone,
Saying, "You've got to hold on"

And though my body aches
My Savior never forsakes,
I thought that I'd be gone,
But He said, "You must hold on"

Though I do know my condition
I won't give up my position,
Jesus sits upon a throne,
He said, "You will hold on."

About the Author

Gloria Murphy Smith was born in St. Augustine, Florida. She lost her parents at a young age and was raised by her grandmother and an aunt who adopted her, along with three siblings.

Gloria grew up facing the challenges of poverty in the south. Her Christian faith has sustained her through many tragic personal events which weighed heavily on her heart. These events caused her great sociological, psychological, and economic stress.

She is a graduate of Jefferson County High School in Monticello. She worked for the States of Florida, California, and Nebraska before becoming disabled. She enjoys writing, reading, teaching young children, and going to family gatherings.

She attributes her knowledge and success to her Lord and Savior, Jesus Christ, and in part to her grandmother, who instilled in her the foundation for becoming a strong and independent woman.

Acknowledgements

I give reverence to my Lord and Savior, Jesus Christ, who is always first and foremost in my life, for blessing me with wisdom and knowledge, and for allowing me to stay healthy enough to complete this book from beginning to end. To Him be the glory.

I'd like to thank my daughter, LaChanda T. Brooks, my son, Marquis D. Brooks, and my precious grandson, Abdul Jabaar Mussington, Jr., for really believing in me and for all of their unconditional love and support. I could not have done it without you.

Thanks to my sisters, Bessie Murphy Gallon, Rosetta Murphy Byrd, and to my brother, Eddie James Murphy, Sr., and the rest of my nieces and nephews, cousins, friends and my sisters and brothers in Christ, for all of their love, along with their words of encouragement and prayers. All of these things were key ingredients to making this book possible. Thanks to several other very special family members, Beverly Byrd, Almedia Byrd Locklear, Anna Grace Virgil, and Reverend Eddie J. Johnson. They were inspirational to me both spiritually and emotionally.

Thanks to my publisher, Barbara Joe-Williams, for believing in me from the moment we met, and for allowing me the opportunity to pursue my dream. I have learned so many good and wonderful things just by being in your presence.

I'd also like to thank Dr. Willie Tillman Williams, Thelma S. Washington, and Lois Carolyn Graham for their love and support and for all words of encouragement. Thanks to a very special friend in Los Angeles, California, Dr. Vera J. Roberts, for all of your many phone calls, suggestions, prayers, words of encouragement, and for having so much faith in me. Thanks to all the readers of "Mirror to the Soul of a Woman" and to every one who desire to purchase and read this book of poems. I truly believe that you will enjoy and cherish these poems forever. Thanks to everyone else whose name may not appear at this time, but are forever embedded in my memory and in my heart. GOD BLESS!

151

Printed in the United States
112198LV00007B/333/A